GWS

GROW WITH SNOW

VISION

BEST ADVICE FOR ENTREPRENEURS

GWS
GROW WITH SNOW

Michelle Snow

ABOUT THE AUTHOR

GWS
GROW WITH SNOW

Michelle Snow

Michelle Snow is the Platinum Connect & Vision to Performance Coach formerly known as "Career Coach on Duty". She is a Philanthropist, Award Winning Coach, the President & Executive Consultant of multiple companies, and Founder of the non-profit "Grow Together Snow Foundation". Today, Michelle and her companies continue to stretch its borders. She's not only an Executive Business Coach, Michelle serves as an expert in Visionary Leadership & Professional Growth for educational institutions, corporations, and businesses. Michelle is recognized by FORBES, Philadelphia City Council, Philadelphia Department of Commerce, and multiple major media. Michelle offers years of professional employment experience through national and multi-national corporations. During her career, she interfaced with colleagues of all levels. Michelle's corporate, community, and education experience provides her with leverage to serve clients and community as a benchmark in people-growth, strategy, and development. Michelle's passion is best expressed through her personal mantra, "Living Epistles Grow Together".

DEDICATIONS

GWS
GROW WITH SNOW

This book is dedicated to…

My Mother – My Queen and Love of My Life! My warrior, faith, sword, and delight. You are God's gift and I love you forever.

Cardell – My Sweetheart who always believed I was an author. Thank you for not being jealous of my schedule and supporting the shenanigans of this butterfly.

Aunt Marsha – For telling me my skirt was too short, being my first employee, and my at-home minister.

Every Prospect that Said No – You passed over or rejected me. Thank you! Because of you I learned to believe in myself. I learned that NO is an acronym for Next Opportunity.

Every Company that Fired Me – Thank you for releasing me at the divine and appointed time. The timing and swift decision making worked in divine order.

My First Grade Teacher – Who taught me how to read a dictionary and helped my second-grade teacher have patience with me.

GOD – I am a follower of the Lord Jesus Christ! God is my source, provider and comforter. Our supporters, clients and members receive services driven by biblical principles.

Dedication to WENGP
Women's Energy Network of Greater Philadelphia

"May strength, courage and power comfort, carry and equip you! You are divine light and energy! As we enter this next new season, I confirm miracles. Your dreams will awaken your potential. You now take intentional action steps quickly. No longer will you be bound or tied to circumstances, policies, people or principles that delay God's divine plan for your life. You are the answer you are seeking! Peace is your decision. I declare that you decide now!

Finally, WENGP, as women in leadership, it is still necessary that we remember LOVE covers a multitude of faults. It's our time to forgive others and ourselves. Living Epistles MUST Grow Together"

Sincerely,
Michelle Snow
www.growwithsnow.com

TABLE OF CONTENTS

HAVANA BOOK GROUP LLC
2173 SALK AVE, SUITE 250
CARLSBAD, CA. 92008

COPYRIGHT 2022 All rights reserved.
ISBN: 979-8-9862647-5-2

INTRODUCTION

GWS
GROW WITH SNOW

How To Use This Book

Dear Leader, Entrepreneur, Business and Person of Influence…

God called you out! I believed in you, your abilities, your resilience, your character, and your strength long before I knew we would meet. Years ago after being removed (downsized) from a global corporate company, I saw you in a dream. The Creator revealed your possibilities. May I encourage you?

> "Never Give Up Too Soon!"
> *(Unknown Author)*

The most difficult obstacles you must overcome are the lies you told yourself before today.

This custom book of stories, examples, and notes are *SPLASH (quick bold and refreshing)* Conversations to help rising leaders fill your knowledge gap. The notes are not a storyline.

You may Skim, Speed Read, Focus on a Topic, Review at Your Leisure, or Relax and Read the FULL Book Straight through!

Ultimately, consider it like a cheat sheet or pocket guide as you…

Launch, Land and Grow!

Notes and Reflections

_____

_____

_____

_____

_____

_____

_____

_____

_____

_____

_____

_____

_____

_____

_____

_____

CHAPTER 1

GWS
GROW WITH SNOW

GETTING STARTED

Getting started can be difficult; don't panic! The following are tips for first-time emerging leaders who are just getting started or thinking about launching a business, leading an enterprise in transition organizations, or faith-groups seeking visionary tools for their front-line leaders. There are many pitfalls that may be avoided. This list outlines behaviors to be aware of as you embark on your exciting new journey. Consider this a checklist of suggested Do's & Do Not's. It will help you launch or pivot with the best possibility for success!

Steps for Success

1. **Work (Exercise) Your Mindset!** FAITH - Find scripture, affirmations, and videos to help you change your thinking. Literally, you have to change your thought process from an employee to an owner, seer, and visionary. Les Brown, T.D. Jakes, and Bob Proctor are highly recommended; they were instrumental in changing my thinking. You may also want to read/research articles about neuroscience and human behavior. Spirit and science matter; they work together.

2. **Do Not Invest Too Much Time Watching Others!** Do not become an obsessive-addictive copy of others. Seek your inner voice (spirit) for your path. Embrace your own destiny! Accept that you are designed to offer, render, deliver and serve an audience prepared specifically for the brilliance and magic within you. You are the special order!

3. **Position Yourself as a Thought Leader / Influencer!** Show the world that your experience, hardships, productivity, planning, investments, discoveries and education matter. How? Write articles, blogs, podcasts, letters, email campaigns, video storytelling, text and live call campaigns, along with FREE or affordable eBook and paper books. Professional, credible social media is critical to your success (i.e. LinkedIn, YouTube, Twitter, Facebook, Instagram, etc.).

4. **Create a Product or Service Quickly!** Get familiar with being responsible for a "thing." You must learn how to create, launch, and manage your own systems. Whether it's a T-Shirt, coffee mug, PDF download, class, essential or vanity product, network marketing, or affiliate services, do it quickly! Learn to be accountable and responsible for your own branding, content, marketing and packaging. Practice is necessary! Do not depend on vendors too soon. Find easy apps and DIY sites. Become comfortable with money so that the energy of money will become comfortable with you.

5. **Do NOT Wait for Perfection!** Entrepreneurs always start flawed. It's the unspoken norm. Countless leading-brands sell and promise a service before it's ready for manufacturing or distribution. Sorry to burst your bubble, but that's the truth. You must work ferociously to have an excellent execution strategy so that your promise is credible and not fraudulent. Start with an excellent Launch System.

"The Pessimist Sees Difficulty in Every Opportunity
The Optimist Sees Opportunity in Every Difficulty."
(Winston Churchill)

Self-Reflection

1. Work (Exercise) Your Mindset!
List 3 things you will do starting today to work on your mindset.

_____

_____

_____

2. Do Not Invest Too Much Time Watching Others!
List 3 things you are going to do to embrace your destiny.

_____

_____

_____

3. Position Yourself as a Thought Leader / Influencer!
List 3 ways you are going to position yourself as a thought leader.

_____

_____

_____

4. Create a Product or Service Quickly!
What new product or service will you create in the next 30 days?

_____

_____

_____

_____

5. Do NOT Wait for Perfection!
How will you launch your new product or service?

_____

_____

_____

_____

_____

_____

_____

CHAPTER 2

LAUNCH FAIL

Failure is not final. No one likes to fail, but do not be afraid of the fall. There are many examples of businesses that have failed when launching new products. Some of these are iconic companies that were in business for a while, yet failed in a product launch. Nevertheless, they still found a way to keep the business going despite failure and/or embarrassment. Here are examples:

Harley Davidson
- Company: Harley Davidson
- Year: 1994
- Product: Perfume

Harley Davidson was known as one of the most iconic and valuable brands in the world. It is also one of the most masculine brands. In earlier years, the company did not deviate considerably from this manly personality, although it has tried. The company released Legendary Harley-Davidson, a cologne for men in 1994. Another perfume, Black Fire, hit the market in 2005. All are now discontinued. In the 1990s, the company released a number of other products, including wine coolers and aftershave, which after failing miserably have also become classic cases of brand overextension. Sauter, Comen, Frohlich and Stebbins (2018) give more information in their article, *When Product Launches Go Awry.*

Heinz

- Company: Heinz
- Year: 2000
- Product: EZ Squirt

Before EZ Squirt, ketchup was always varying shades of red. To cater to kids, who were -- and still are -- among ketchup's largest groups of consumers, Heinz began producing purple, green, and blue EZ Squirt ketchup in matching, vibrantly colored squeeze bottles. At first, the colorful ketchup was a huge success. The novelty soon wore off, and not long after its introduction, sales of EZ Squirt began to decline. In January 2006, less than six years after its debut, Heinz halted production of the product.

This is an example where the launch was a welcomed new way of lifestyle eating. Heinz experienced over five years of success with children and families. Perhaps they faced blind spots.

Here are Points to Consider:

- Did Heinz ignore declining sales prior to the total loss of the product line? Why or Why not

_____

_____

_____

_____

_____

_____

- Was it possible to transition to treating the product as a limited edition or holiday condiment? Why or Why not

_____

_____

_____

_____

- Did they forget to notice that their primary target audience was aging?

_____

_____

_____

- Does a 10-year-old child to age 15 still enjoy colorful ketchup? Why or Why Not?

_____

_____

_____

- Is the child-customer still eating home cooked meals with family after five years? Why or Why not?

_____

_____

_____

- Is colorful ketchup available through commercial (retail food chains) dining experiences? Why or Why not?

_____

_____

_____

- Did the economy slow down which in turn motivated parents to purchase competing affordable choices? Why or Why not?

_____

_____

_____

- Did Heinz know the value of trend and seasonal (i.e. Ugly Christmas Sweaters or a Patty Pie) products vs permanent products? Why or Why not?

_____

_____

_____

_____

_____

_____

CHAPTER 3

GWS
GROW WITH SNOW

CAPABILITY STATEMENT

If you are a new, aspiring or grassroots leader, you will likely NOT be required to present a capability statement to your new or potential clients. As you grow, here is a great practice tool to help you learn how to identify your strengths early on in your organization or business' growth and development.

In addition, it will help you plan for achieving higher goals as you grow. The capability statement will include, but is not limited to the following items:

1. Company name
2. Company address and contact information
3. Core competencies
4. Brief company overview
5. Customer description
6. Government codes and certifications
7. Number of years in business
8. Primary services description
9. Unique Value Proposition (UVP)
10. Business references

Staffing Solutions of Hawaii
1357 Kapiolani Blvd. Suite 1410
Honolulu, Hawaii, 96814
P: (808) 949-3669
F: (808) 949-4022

Staffing Solutions
OF HAWAII
Joining People

We are proud to be an Equal
Employment Opportunity and Affirmative
Action employer, including females,
minorities, protected Veterans, and
those with disability.

CAPABILITY STATEMENT

Originated in 1991, Staffing Solutions of Hawaii is an elite-staffing firm conveniently located in Honolulu, Hawaii. Serving as the access point for employee placement and government contracts, SSOH is committed to providing top-quality **direct hire, temp-to-hire, temporary, and payroll services**. From entry-level to upper level management, the company specializes in office and administrative positions in a variety of industries.

ACCOUNTING & FINANCE
Accountant, Accounting Clerk, Accounts Payable/Receivable, Billing Clerk, Bookkeeper, Compensation Analyst, CPA, Payroll Professionals, Senior Accountant, Tax Accountant

ADMINISTRATIVE
Administrative Assistant, Claims Examiner/Processor, Clerk, Data Entry, File Clerk, Human Resources Assistant, Management Assistant, Receptionist, Typist, Underwriter

CUSTOMER SERVICE
Account Representative, Call Center Operations, Customer Service Representative, Customer Service Specialist, Enrollment Representative, Provider Claims Representative

EXECUTIVE PLACEMENT
Chief Executive Officer, Chief Financial Officer, Chief Operating Officer, Director, Vice President

INFORMATION TECHNOLOGY
Business Analyst, CISSP Professionals, Database Support, EHR Implementation Specialist, Engineers, Help Desk Support, HRIS Analyst, Network Engineers & Technicians, Systems Analyst

MANAGEMENT
Human Resources Manager, Lean Six Sigma Consultants, Office Manager, Project Manager, Recruitment Manager, Tax Manager

For additional information about Staffing Solutions of Hawaii's capabilities, please contact our office at (808) 949-3669 or email us at ssoh@staffingsolutionsofhawaii.com. Visit our website at www.staffingsolutionsofhawaii.com to learn more.

Company Information

TIN: 99-0307054

DUNS: 807470539

CAGE Code: 1ST33

GSA Contract No.: GS-07F-0169N

GSA Certification: 15+ Years

Contract Expiration: November 30, 2017

NAICS Codes:

561320 Temporary Help Services (Primary)

561110 Office Administrative Services

561311 Employment Placement Agencies

561312 Executive Search Services

561499 All Other Business Support Services

Secret Clearance

Business References

AlohaCare

American Savings Bank

HMSA

Kamehameha Schools

Matson Terminals

Servco Pacific Inc.

University Health Alliance

1. Your Company Name

_____

2. Your Company Address and Contact Information

_____

_____

_____

3. Your Core Competencies

_____

_____

_____

_____

4. Your Company Overview

_____

_____

_____

_____

5. Your Ideal Customer Description

_____

_____

_____

_____

_____

_____

6. Government Codes and Certifications

_____

_____

_____

_____

_____

_____

7. Number of Years You have been in Business

_____

8. Your Primary Services Description

_____

_____

_____

9. Unique Value Proposition (UVP)

_____

_____

_____

_____

10. Business References

_____

_____

_____

_____

_____

Notes and Reflections

CHAPTER 4

GWS
GROW WITH SNOW

NEW INITIATIVES

It takes great courage to manifest a vision to performance. Only the courageous and the outrageous will survive. In the face of fear, courage says, "I will do it despite how I feel or how I think." Outrageous says, "Even though it appears ridiculous, I am definitely doing it!"

Daily Clarity Techniques
Here are tools to escort you on this journey of greatness. Below are four (4) keys to greatness from the book by Les Brown, *"Greatness is in You."*

1. Prayer and Meditation

In an effort to build your masterpiece, keep cleansing your mind and your spirit. Continue to commit quiet time at the start of your day reading inspiration. In your quiet time, imagine yourself functioning in your business. What you can see, you can make real. Speak daily affirmations of confidence, health, courage, strength, wealth, favor, grace and ability.

The mind is your invisible key to unlock or destroy your future. It will both unlock and lock your destiny. Use the mind with care and exhaustive imagination.

2. Sketch, White Board, Goal Card and Journal the Vision

Some call it a vision board. Keep a pad that is exclusive to your business dreams and goals (preferably paper and digital). As you see new ideas and concepts in your heart, write them or draw them on your **Sketch, White Board, Goal Card and Journal Book.** There will be times when your mind is flooded with ideas. You will not be able to contain everything within the location of new memories in your brain. Also, write down the date of the conversation, dream, moment of spark, passion or insight. When you cannot write, record your thoughts verbally in your phone (digital device).

3. Guard Your Ears and Eyes

Your body is a living breathing temple from your Divine Creator. You have unique abilities and powers that cannot be duplicated. Your vision is your spiritual download that impacts the minds, hearts and lifestyle of generations. Be conscious of how you visually and audibly entertain yourself. Your music, conversations or entertainment have the ability to be both damaging and/or helpful to your next move.

4. Forgive

Any person or circumstance that you hold hostage to your bitterness, resentment, or anger, PLEASE STOP! You cannot be great with these internal blockages. Forgiveness does not indicate weakness. You may only be able to mask your rage and negative emotions temporarily before you implode. Forgive your adversary quickly! Do this even though you are right! Forgiveness is not a greenlight to reengage your adversary. It is only a pathway to fill your pain with something more positive and productive. Let it go, now. Close the door. #FaithUp

Notes and Reflections

_____

_____

_____

_____

_____

_____

_____

_____

_____

_____

_____

_____

_____

_____

_____

_____

Notes and Reflections

CHAPTER 5

GET A COACH

Overview of Working with a Coach
For Your Strategy

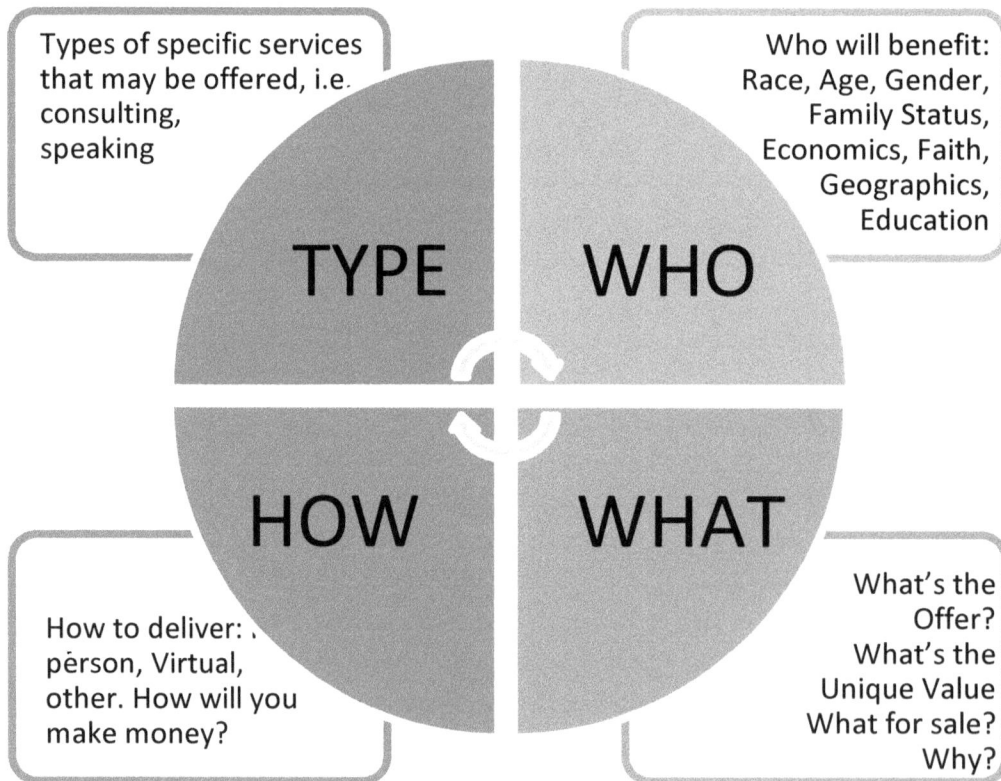

Types of specific services that may be offered, i.e. consulting, speaking

Who will benefit: Race, Age, Gender, Family Status, Economics, Faith, Geographics, Education

TYPE

WHO

HOW

WHAT

How to deliver: person, Virtual, other. How will you make money?

What's the Offer? What's the Unique Value What for sale? Why?

Growth Planning Stages for the Visionary or Owner! Here are the main stages to help you identify your growth-position in your business industry and within the domestic or global the economy.

1. **Embryonic – Idea, Imagination, and Creative Stage.** It is too soon for historic data. This is the research and data gathering phase. It requires building relationships and creating brand awareness. This is the time for saving money, learning the criteria for bank & micro lending, credit readiness, as well as grassroots initiatives and deliverables. Writing a business plan is essential. At this stage your confidence is likely weak even though the vision may be strong.

2. **Emerging – Building Confidence, Measuring Performance, and Skill Strengthening.** You are working, measuring and executing your business plan as well as starting a strategic plan. You are learning to delegate, hire and trust others. You embrace the thrill of momentum and enthusiasm with your new fans and consumers. You may be working from home or shared work space and wearing many hats, i.e. customer care, administration, marketing, bookkeeping, shipping, or perhaps more roles.

3. **Established – You Are Better Positioned to Predict Data, Pay Yourself and Others.** Your business generates consistent on-going sales, you've learned to NOT panic when the company has roadblocks, setbacks, crisis, embarrassment or loss. You are no longer committed to only working with people you know. You now have organizational standards and norms. Automation is necessary for you, and you now see efficiency within your operation functions.

4. **Highly Established** – You now have the confidence teach and mentor others to replace you. You are now preparing your legacy. You are scaling for growth or your exit strategy. You are considering mergers and acquisitions. You have mastered multiple income streams. The company is generating income with or without your physical presence. You likely have manufacturing within the business framework.

Other STAGES in Business

STAGE – Financial and Bankability

1. Launch – Possible Debt, Promised Sales, Feeling Overwhelmed
2. Maturation – Learning Internal Systems, Paid Consistently
3. Explosive – Mastered a Marketing Niche Trend, Feeling Rich
4. Plateau – Holding Your Position, Moved from Rich to Wealthy
5. Acquisition – Ready to Start Something New or Retire

STAGE – Staff, Team and Employee

1. Form - Newly Hired, Onboarding, Forming Relationships
2. Launch – Close of New-Hire Stage, Now Adding Value
3. Opposition – Learning to Resolve Conflicts or Deficiencies
4. Stabilization – Consistent Measurable Performance
5. Peak – Consistent Peak Performance and Significant Leadership

Important: As you evolve, expand, fail and maintain your vision, these stages will relapse and repeat. You are never 100% locked into any stage ever. Why? The unpredictability of people, your purpose and the market place is life's wildcard. Technology and artificial intelligence will not predict everything. The God factor continues.

Growth Planning Stages for the Visionary or Owner!

Notes and Reflection

_____

_____

_____

_____

_____

_____

_____

_____

_____

_____

_____

_____

_____

_____

_____

CHAPTER 6

SERVICE PROFESSIONALS

Planning as service professionals such as speakers, trainers, and coaches, please note, the order of the action steps are determined by the business owner. Below are examples of where and how to invest in the initial phase of an aggressive vision launch (approximately 90 Days).

Content Writing

- Design your content to fit your target audience. Sensitivity to gender, experience, culture, age, education and economics are important. Your content and programs must speak to the audience you are attracting and most importantly to those that are paying you for service.

_____

_____

_____

_____

_____

- When writing content, you must note your mode of delivery. Consider both live in-person engagement and digital. Be mindful that your service mode may be offered as a hybrid, i.e. on-line, pre-recorded, video and through live calls. A hybrid model will help you stay flexible and adjust to multiple client types and the changing culture and economy. Ultimately, you will decide on your most dominant mode of delivery based upon customer demand.

Market Research and Brand Planning

- What is the relevance of what you are doing, selling, or servicing? Why is it important? Does it solve a problem? What are you prepared to do to inspire your audience to feel like they need what you are offering? Who are the key leaders (stakeholders) in your industry? What contributes to your industry's success? What are your costs (budget)? What are your peers or competitors charging for a similar service?

_____

_____

_____

_____

_____

_____

_____

_____

_____

_____

_____

_____

_____

_____

- Where (apps, platform, physical place) will you deliver this service or product? What tools are available to help you deliver this service or product?

_____

_____

_____

_____

_____

- Are you able to manage this vision on your own (solo)? Why or Why not?

_____

_____

_____

_____

_____

_____

_____

_____

- As a leader or business owner, you require a profile, not a resume. Inform your network that you are a subject matter expert. Resumes are for jobs. Profiles are necessary and excellent to demonstrate your independent accomplishments.

The Event/Reveal Design!

- When designing events, design the scope of activities, i.e. what happens as the guests arrive, how the guests interact during the event and how the event is expected to close. Consider the guests pre-networking and post-networking (if relevant) experience.

- Be clear about the event perks, benefits and rewards.

_____

_____

_____

_____

_____

The Pilot: Test Run / Soft Launch

- Host your first activity, i.e. event, workshop, class, conversation, meet-up, etc. Do something with a small group in your target audience and request feedback from the participants about the experience. This is recommended to help you experience the effectiveness of your leadership capacity and ability to draw or attract followers to support or buy from you. This is the start of your market analysis and data gathering.

_____

_____

_____

_____

_____

_____

_____

_____

1. Pre-Marketing – How to Attract Sales or Connections

- Flyers, social media, e-blast (CRM), paid promotion, word of mouth, referrals, testimonials, traditional media, texts, live calls, partnership sites, ambassador/influencers, VIP invitation only, pre-paid block tickets honoring your favorite cause/charity, network with other virtual or live events to build trust and awareness. Create alliances and partnerships.

_____

_____

_____

_____

_____

2. Live Marketing – What To Do

- Stream the activity and post live mini video clips and pictures. Ask guests to hashtag their experience or testimonial. Offer pre-pay or pre-sale discounts for future services or products. Give live surveys through games or app questionnaires, and customer retargeting.

_____

_____

_____

_____

- For products that are shipped, when consumers open the product, what is the intended emotional experience?

_____

_____

_____

_____

_____

Is the package colorful or inspirational? Does the product work and in excellent condition? Did the package arrive on-time? Did the package include all promises or instructions?

_____

_____

_____

_____

_____

- Customer Service: If the consumer requires assistance during a live activity or service, what is the quality of your response?

_____

_____

_____

_____

- When receiving complaints about a shipment, is your customer service compassionate, empathetic, relational, and or effective?

_____

_____

_____

_____

_____

3. Post Marketing – What to Say, Share or Do After the Sale
- Similar to post production, post marketing / post care are critical. Consumers will chat online, at home, at functions, on texts, in the halls, at social locations, or in the digital world about the experience they had with your product or service. Your reputation never sleeps. Work on a positive brand name, but be ready to rebound from negativity quickly. Note: Strategies for passive or residual income may or may not be applicable for the above.

_____

_____

_____

_____

_____

_____

_____

Why Data from Your Launch May be Inaccurate

- Consumers may flood your grand opening because of grassroots momentum.
- Consumers are eager to experience a new opportunity.
- Your marketing triggered a spending/investment sensor with your audience, however there was no long-term need for the service.
- The product was too good! There was no short-term need for a second purchase, maintenance, or follow-up. You OVER Delivered!
- The product or service did not live up to the hype, perception, or marketing message.
- The product or service was a fad, trend or seasonal purchase.
- Your consumer online reviews were awful, or your competitors sabotaged you by posting abundant fake negative reviews.
- After your launch or opening, a competitor copied the product or service, mastered marketing it, and sold it for less.
- Too Advanced! Consumers were intimidated by the branding or technology. The product is too luxurious or too advanced for consumer desires. They don't understand your offer and cannot appreciate your intended benefits.
- Your systems to collect and track data or consumer experience may be weak or fragile. You may have data errors. Invest in stronger technology.
- Loss, theft, charge-backs, returns and exchanges were not yet identified. This happens when you discover fraud. Invest in surveillance and tracking systems. Those you initially trusted may require tighter security or you must remove staff or allies from their designated position(s). Also, prepare for an online security breach, i.e. cyber-attack or hack.
- Damaged products, or unsatisfactory service may lead to refunds.

CHAPTER 7

GWS
GROW WITH SNOW

KEY REMINDERS AS YOU GROW

As you grow, there are certain things you do to help facilitate continued growth. Growth does not happen automatically. You may consider the following.

Content Plan
- What are you saying, doing, sharing and the dates?

_____

_____

_____

_____

Brand Perception
- Is it fun, reliable, strong, serious, cutting edge, lasting, etc.?

_____

_____

_____

_____

Social and Digital, Print, Other Media
- What platforms are your priority and deliver best results?

_____

_____

_____

_____

Profile and Relationships
- Business profile, partnerships, followers and fans

_____

_____

_____

_____

Financial Fitness
- Personal credit is the gateway to business credit. Your personal credit will help you get business funding.

_____

_____

_____

_____

- Where's the Money? Once you master approximately $5,000 a month in income, and have a satisfactory credit score, you are a candidate for credit and cash financing (loans). Visit Micro Lenders such as, PayPal, Square, KIVA, Crowd Funders, CDFIs, etc. Grants are also excellent, and typically no credit score is required.

Quick Income

- Design sellable tools to provide you with both credibility and income resources, i.e. books, merchandising, classes, etc.

_____

_____

_____

_____

_____

Identify Consumer Behavior / Client Avatar

- "Consumer behavior is the study of how individual customers, groups or organizations select, buy, use, and dispose ideas, goods, and services to satisfy their needs and wants. It refers to the actions of the consumers in the marketplace and the underlying motives for those actions."

_____

_____

_____

_____

_____

_____

_____

- Understanding Buyer Behavior: Once you begin to analyze the data, you can begin to make assessments about your consumers and target market. The history of their buying patterns will show you where and what you can predict for future products and services.

_____

_____

_____

_____

_____

- A customer avatar is a detailed profile of your ideal customer. It doesn't make assumptions or categorize people into groups. The avatar focuses on one person and outlines everything about him or her. It goes into much greater depth than a regular marketing persona, providing marketers with many more targeting tools.
  - Personal Habits
  - Lifestyle needs and desires (Travel, etc.)
  - Points of pain, pleasure, personal triggers (Likes or Dislikes)
  - Types of affiliations and memberships
  - Spiritual or religious norms

_____

_____

_____

_____

_____

Notes and Reflections

CHAPTER 8

GWS
GROW WITH SNOW

COMPELLING MONEY MESSAGE (CMM)

What Every Leader and Business Owner Must Know and Master!

Congratulations on using your gifts and talents to increase your income and help others reach their goals through your vision! Now, it's time that you prepare to profit and propel your revenue potential in an upward direction.

Your money is waiting for YOU to CLAIM it, but first, you must know how to COMMAND it. That's where the Compelling Money Message (CMM) comes into play. The CMM should easily answer three questions:

1. How does your business solve problems?

_____

_____

_____

_____

_____

_____

2. What distinguishes you from other businesses, or, what is your unique selling proposition (USP).

_____

_____

_____

_____

_____

3. What experience do you guarantee your customers after working with or buying from you?

_____

_____

_____

_____

_____

_____

Let's say that you are a virtual assistant, specifically for creative entrepreneurs. You will build a client avatar as outlined in the previous chapter in order to create your CMM. It's critical to remember that your CMM should always prioritize the client, which will inevitably yield consistent cash flow for your business.

_____

_____

_____

_____

_____

_____

_____

_____

_____

_____

_____

_____

_____

_____

This is Leslie. She lives in California, is a wife, mother of two toddlers, and has a passion for graphic designing. Although Leslie also has a day job as a Registered Nurse and earns $100K per year, she does not enjoy it. Designing is her stress-reliever and creative outlet. She has a B.A. degree in Graphic Design, but has yet to land her dream job. In the interim, she has done some freelance work for her friends and is ready to turn her passion into profit. Leslie's problem is that she does not have the capacity to correspond with prospective clients, send multiple emails, manage her social media, and craft outstanding graphics.

Even though she has already created a workflow for her onboarding system, she does not have the bandwidth to implement it, and is consequently hindered from delivering an exceptional experience. Her USP (Unique Selling Proposition) includes hand-sketching each design before converting it to a digital file, offering video feedback for each client during the offboarding process, and creating mock-ups that the client can use as branding assets.

Leslie's Brief Client Avatar below…

Wow! Leslie is a graphic-design BOSS! When she isn't working her job or working hard for her business, she squeezes in quality time with her family. Sometimes she gets so busy that she forgets to eat, which causes her to feel burned out. Her hobbies include tennis, pottery, and running marathons. Leslie values time and efficacy over money, meaning she will pay a premium price for convenience. She knows how to relinquish control, doesn't micro-manage, and trusts the experts to deliver on their promise.

Now, due to the stress, Leslie is on the brink of quitting her business, and is in dire need of a virtual assistant. She understands that even solopreneurs must consider outsourcing work. Good News! Now that you've studied Leslie's avatar, this is your opportunity to pitch your CMM to her. It's similar to an elevator pitch, but hones in on how your service or product will maximize the prospect customer.

SAMPLE CMM:

Hi Leslie! I can see that you are a BOSS at graphic design, and I know that you can help businesses upgrade their branding. I am a virtual assistant, and my superpower is helping you to reach your goals by effectively communicating with your clients, organizing your tasks, and guaranteeing that you have the work-life balance that you desire.

The assistance that I can provide ranges from managing your onboarding and offboarding process through a customer relationship management (CRM) software that is specifically developed for digital creatives like yourself and responding to prospective customers' emails to helping you establish a work-routine that helps your creative juices flow as well as scheduling food breaks when you go into overdrive.

I am committed to ensuring that you are successful in servicing your clients. I offer monthly retainer packages, day-rates, and billable hours. You also have the option to book services on-demand. Leslie, I know that time is your most valuable resource, and as your virtual assistant, my aim is to help you reclaim it!

Now it's your turn! I both challenge and urge you to use the above sample to create your own client avatar and CMM to pitch to your demographic and target customer audience.

While your CMM is designed to help you write a profitable message to attract more clients, its primary function is to explain how your clients will profit after working with you. When writing your compelling money message, it's vital that you direct it toward your demographic or target audience. Your demographic or ideal audience is the group of people or industry that you desire to serve.

Newsflash! Everyone isn't your client — and that's okay. The fact is, you actually get more business when you focus on a particular niche. In our example, the demographic is creative people who are remarkable at their craft, but lack project management proficiencies. After identifying your demographic, you can then position yourself as the bridge or solution to their problem and explain how they will benefit from your services.

Defining Your Demographic

Before you solidify the services or products you will provide, outline your Standard Operating Procedures (SOPs), and project your revenue goals. Clarify your demographic to know exactly who to direct your messaging to without wasting time or energy on people who are not in the market for what you have to offer.

If you work best with people or small businesses that are creative geniuses, are unorganized, and rely on you to add structure to their day, then it would behoove you to work with people who need assistance with managing their creative control. Conversely, you may not work well with corporate professionals who micromanage your performance and require you to attend daily meetings. As you discover your strengths and weaknesses, as well as the things you like and don't like to do, then you will learn what type of clients that will fit well within your business.

Confirm your demographic, assess your strengths:

1. What do I do well?

_____

_____

_____

_____

_____

2. What industry and tasks do I naturally enjoy?

_____

_____

_____

_____

3. What are my non-negotiables in a business relationship?

_____

_____

_____

_____

4. What does my ideal client behave like?

_____

_____

_____

_____

_____

_____

_____

5. Why does my ideal client need me?

_____

_____

_____

_____

_____

_____

_____

_____

Your CMM should be two-fold (benefiting you and the client), detailed, solution-oriented, and demographic-specific. Once you clarify your compelling money message, you will experience exponential cash flow in your business!

_____

_____

_____

_____

_____

_____

_____

_____

_____

_____

_____

_____

_____

To Achieve a Dynamic Compelling Money Message

5 CALLS-TO-ACTION

1. Nostalgic Association
- Messaging that reminds the consumer of a time in history or their life of importance, happiness, or a positive permanent memory. This will help them to reconnect with their "why". A person's why or purpose, is the reason they started their venture.
- Leslie may have seen her parents work tirelessly for someone else's dream without ever considering their own ambitions. Maybe she would illustrate to quell depression, which brought her joy. This may have led her to start a company so that she can show her children that one can capitalize off of their creativity while working at a job.

_____

_____

_____

_____

_____

_____

_____

_____

_____

_____

2. Virtual + Brick and Mortar Retail Placement and Visibility

- The Golden Rule in Business: Make it easy for your clients to buy your products or services. To achieve this you will create a workflow to streamline your process for purchases. If you sell products in a big-box store, then the products are expected to be conveniently placed for your customer to reach it.

- Toys marketed to 5-year-olds cannot be shelved on the top shelf! How will they be able to sneak it into their parents' cart? Likewise, if you operate in the e-commerce space, then you will purchase ad (advertising) space that currently and successfully caters to your desired demographic.

- If you market your business by way of a social media influencer, then prepare to research their audience. For instance, if you sell hair products tailored for natural curls, then purchasing ad space on a page that primarily promotes bundle packages of hair may be an utter waste of your marketing budget.

- Position your business to excel by placing it directly in the eyes of your prospective consumers!

3. Pricing

- Underpricing or overcharging is the bane of most businesses. Sticker shock is real, but so is premium value. Do you provide premium value for your clientele, but are paid "Great Value"? If you answered yes, then it's time to re-evaluate your audience, pricing structure, and offerings. Each of these pillars are instrumental in helping you to reach your revenue goals.

- **Audience:** Do you provide a custom, luxury experience for your clients? Leslie, for example, could invest in a CRM that gives her clients a portal or virtual home for their deliverables. By providing sample mockups that her clients can repurpose as marketing assets, she's asserting herself as a premium business. Why? She is offering something that one can purchase and capitalize from for future endeavors. But, does her audience value that enough to pay a premium price for it?

- **Industry Research:** You can determine your prices by researching the price points of your competitors. Once you assess their offerings and compare them to yours, it becomes easier for you to competently and comparably price your services or products.

- **Focus on Your Own Plow:** The bane of pricing is focusing on your value and not your clients' budgets. In other words, stay out of your clients' pockets! If it costs you $10 to create a product, then in order to profit, you will consider a price point at minimum 100% return when possible ($20+). People will purchase and value it because you have positioned it properly. Your CMM is the catalyst for pricing your services and products equitably.

4. Race / Culture

- It's critical for you to remember that the people who look like you, identify as your same gender or race, or have other similarities to you, may not be your ideal client or fit your avatar profile — AND THAT'S OKAY! Your capital may not always reside in your native culture.

Race / Culture continued…

- Be clear on your CMM and client avatar. Prioritize your marketing efforts on the culture that best fits your demographic. For example, the beauty industry is a billion-dollar industry and the Black community at large is its largest revenue generator. However, most of the beauty supply stores are owned and operated by Pacific-Asians or other races although their core client is often African-American or Blacks.

- If your company provides equipment for a hospital or a construction company, then you must tailor your CMM to match the jargon of your potential consumers. Also, if your family or friends aren't purchasing your products or services, do not be so easily offended. Your family, friends or personal circle may not be your target audience. It's also possible they may not be able to afford what you are selling. I suggest that you ask them to refer you to someone you can help.

5. Color Emotion

- Your brand colors are not solely chosen from your personal favorite color palette. Each aspect of your brand, including the logo colors, mood board, etc., will be aligned with your industry and client. McDonald's uses red and yellow to attract its customers because these colors evoke high energy, urgency, happiness, and youth. There is an article on Forbes.com, "Eight Colors That Will Personally Grow Your Personal Brand," that are useful in helping you select your brand colors (Chan, 2019). Determine what emotions you expect your customers to feel when they shop with you. Then select the appropriate colors to achieve that goal and customer outcome.

Boundaries in Your Business

Setting boundaries in your business will help you to reclaim your time and peace of mind. Some people may think that enforcing business hours (times / days that you agree to communicate with clients), contracts, terms and conditions, and other binding agreements are mean, doing too much, or not trusting the client. In reality, agreements and policies protect you as an individual, your business, and your client or customer. Allow me to paint a picture:

A client contracts you to create a logo for their business. They give you complete creative control. They tell you to deliver it whenever you have the time. So, you do just that. You take three months to complete the project, they have multiple edits or revisions that take away your enthusiasm to complete the logos, they are consistently late on payment because there is no written agreement on how or when payments will be accepted, and most importantly, you don't properly wrap the project. By not successfully wrapping or ending the project, you inadvertently permit the client to contact you about amending their deliverables no matter how long it's been since you've given them the final draft. DON'T DO IT TO YOURSELF!

Classic Mistakes of Client Contracts or Agreements:
- Allowing customers to manipulate your prices
- Assuming that your clients are aware of everything you are offering them. The contract is the legal agreement of expectation. The progress update outlines accomplishments.
- Offer an extended grace period for service delivery that hurts your ability to freely serve other clients.
- Not knowing the difference between a client and a customer. They are essentially the same. However, clients typically have a vested long term value (LTV) in your product or service and their spending habits are usually more luxurious and high priced.

Here is an example of how the working relationship should commence and conclude. We will use Leslie as the service provider.

Leslie: Hi, Customer! Thank you so much for reaching out to us for graphic design services.

6. *Please tell me a bit about your company, its values, and what the logo should represent.*
7. *What colors do you plan to use? Don't know? Here's a guide that helps you to choose brand colors based on how you expect the client to feel. (Send them color wheel example)*

Thank you for sharing your vision with me. It will take 7-10 business days to complete the logo. I will begin designing after you have paid a fifty percent deposit as well as provide the information needed to begin the logo. Afterward, we will meet once during the working window, if necessary, to discuss your ideas. I respond to all inquiries within 24-48 business days, Monday to Friday, between 9am and 6pm. Please review the contract which outlines our engagement.

Contract Details
- *Once the logo is completed, I will email you the draft. You will have 3-5 business days to submit any revisions for one edit, if the edits aren't submitted during that time, then it is assumed that you are satisfied with the drafts, which will serve as the final draft. If request amendments to your logo after the editing window has closed, then a project reopen fee will be incurred. Payments submitted more than seven (7) days after the drafts are completed are subject to a late fee. Please sign this contract to acknowledge that you agree to the terms and conditions.*

Feel free to copy and paste this example to help you set boundaries in your business. Please remember, you are responsible for the terms that you initiate. Clients can rightfully use them against you. Always seek an attorney to finalize your legal documents.

Notes and Reflections

CHAPTER 9

GWS
GROW WITH SNOW

FRAUD INFLUENCER

**What Every Leader and Business Owner
Must Know and Master!**

Fraud influencers who disguise as business owners are often people who create and showboat a facade lifestyle that is glamorized and seemingly attainable — but only accessible to common people if they pay the said influencer. Social media has ignited a sense of instant gratification through multiple mediums, but entrepreneurship seems to be the new dominant platform to manipulate and trap new victims.

Many fraud influencers flaunt luxury cars, private jets, international vacations, paid invoices or charts of accounts of large profits, expensive jewelry, and pictures with other influencers or celebrities. They are often caught selling a false lifestyle to vulnerable people and make a living by offering mediocre non-scalable business education or a hyper spirituality and an inflated relationship with their God.

Scenario - If you are invited to a networking event or an exclusive meet-up, then promptly pushed you to purchase or join a program membership to be motivated, empowered, or inspired, but the influencer cannot provide tangible evidence, then the person may be a fraud influencer. Sometimes the exchange isn't always money driven. The influencer may be motivated by power, control and sometimes even deviant sex. If your point of entry or bond into the community is founded on sexual intimacy, violence, bullying, impairment, unethical treatment or anything that leads to a false sense of self and personal security, you may be under the guise of a fraud influencer.

How to spot a fraud influencer or digital scammer? They manifest in many forms. This person may be a friend, family member, neighbor, boss, pastor, spiritual leader, or acquaintance. They are cunning, patient, visionary, and personify themselves as brilliant. They prey on your trust, lack of community, pain or your ignorance.

Fraud influencers invest time and money into their victims (prey). While the victim is in awe of the investment of money or accolades by the influencer, they are studying both your weaknesses and your brilliance. Why? The influencer is seeking your essence, your natural abilities. No investment is too extreme for this schemer. They either want to become you, control you or steal you. Not just your stuff, they want your spirit, energy, mindset, thought process, courage, your hope, AND your stuff. This fraud may be disguised as a helper or superfan. They are highly skilled in getting close to the head decision-maker. Like a chameleon, they will attempt to blend in the background for long durations. They watch, wait, and attempt to profit from your vulnerability. Sometimes they do not desire to directly harm or strip the victim. Their intention is to literally copy you. Copying is NOT necessarily a form of flattery.

How does a fraud influencer spot victims? The victim appears to be alone, vulnerable, desperate, perhaps broken. They also tend to be exceptionally talented. The fraud influencer listens to your pain, dreams and appears to be understanding. What you don't often realize is they are simply calculating how to use your words and information against you. Some say fraud influencers demonstrate gaslighting, narcissist tendencies or other personality disorders.

A Typical Fraud Influencer May:
- Possess irrational soaring emotions such as sadness to rage, love to heartless, intensely distracted, overly calculated
- Exaggerate their wealth, intellect and expertise; known liars
- Be attracted to genuine kind people, desire to arrest innocence
- Believe they are the victim; everyone is against them
- Apologize to manipulate people, incapable of genuine remorse
- Seek fear-based people, require isolation of their victim

Fraud Influencers are shameless! They rinse and repeat this vicious cycle listed in the bullets from victim to victim.

How do you maintain your integrity and good ethics in your business or organization?

_____

_____

_____

_____

_____

_____

_____

_____

_____

_____

_____

_____

_____

How to Avoid a Fraud Influencer

To avoid fraud influencers, it's essential that you research credible professionals in the industry. Before purchasing an expensive program or digital product from them, invest in their book, downloadable product or free online videos. Unfortunately, sometimes, testimonials may be staged and fabricated by their super fans. Do your due diligence on the results of the program or item they are selling or showcasing. Always ask yourself, do their programs meet my short-term or long term goals? How?

Also, when possible, interview them. Ask them why they are interested in helping you. If the response is empty, a deflection or self-absorbed, that may be a sign to run! A fraud influencer ultimately seeks to glorify themselves. It is pertinent that you stand firm to develop a reciprocal and equitable connection.

Get to know their leadership style, and determine if it aligns with how you desire to be coached, mentored or led. The primary results based upon leadership styles are typically in two forms; transactional and transformational.

- **Transactional Leaders** emphasize tangible measurable goals, and typically expect to see a determined return on your investment, not necessarily instant gratification. They may render a reward and punishment system to communicate progress or regress in subordinates, members, clients, followers. Their strength is in their ability to react with practical reasoning.

- **Transformational Leaders** highlight the organization's vision, and often include input from team members to create the vision. They promote inclusivity versus isolation. These leaders hone in on the ethos and cultural aspect of their team members or subordinates with enthusiasm and morale. Transformational Leaders are proactive and consider ethics and character in their decision making. They are not jealous nor controlling.

Don't Make Excuses for Them:

- It is important that as leaders we do not excuse bad behavior for the sake of personal stimulation. Fraud influencers are typically very charismatic. They pick and choose victims wisely and cautiously. They often have an excellent reputation with positive people such as medical doctors, people of influence, and political people of power to prove their brand credibility.

- You may not know you are working with a fraud influencer until you are burned, bitten or experienced a loss. They may be slow, methodical and intentional to hunt and stalk their prey. Just because they are positive influences in your life, does not actually mean that he or she or they were a positive influence.

Call me Dad or Mom:

- Does the person manipulate you to refer to them as Mom or Dad? Be careful when early into the connection or relationship if they belittle you by calling you daughter or one of their children. This is a trait used by many to lower your guard by positioning you emotionally to see them as a non-threat and authority figure.

Prophesy for Foretelling:

- Sometimes religious or faith-based communities focus on spiritual hope. They are often caught identifying themselves as God's clear source of news for your future life. They might promise you wealth, marriage, babies, and other things especially if they know you are poor or experiencing financial stress.

Isolation:
- They prefer to isolate you from loved-ones to further manipulate you and destroy both your confidence and personal circle of influence.

Pause and Reflect

_____

_____

_____

_____

_____

_____

_____

_____

_____

_____

_____

_____

_____

_____

_____

Fraud Influencers Lessons to Learn

Every bad experience has a shining light. There are transferrable skills in all learning experiences:

- Recover from emotional challenges more quickly.
- Pace your relationships. Watch before deep personal commitments.
- Be empathic! Less quick to judge others recovering from broken relationships. Listening is no longer enough. Watch and pray.
- Be private and confidential about your personal business while establishing the connection.
- Create and participate in great working cultures in your business, organization or community.
- No experience is wasted. All of it is necessary for your journey.

_____

_____

_____

_____

_____

_____

_____

_____

_____

Notes and Reflections

CHAPTER 10

GWS
GROW WITH SNOW

MOTH EFFECT & IMPACT

"Moth to Flame, Burned by the Fire"
Janet Jackson

I didn't know! It was a surprise to me to learn that a moth was like a fraternal twin of the butterfly. They both often go through the same growth process until the last stage.

The last stage of a butterfly during development is the time it rebirths through the caterpillar cocoon. A butterfly is born usually in less than 14 days. A moth is born usually in less than 21 days.

A moth does something seemingly strange. They are in complete contrast to a butterfly. Instead of completing its final process on a plant in light above ground, a moth dives into the ground and completes its development process in the dirt and darkness. The moth has a unique set of characteristics. These characteristics are excellent tools to help you as you engage leaders, entrepreneurs, business owners, decision makers, people of influence, religious leaders, community activists, and other important partnerships.

Moth Effect & Impact Characteristics

- Out of Season
- Unattractive
- Slippery
- Excellent Night Vision
- Blend in the Background
- Great Pretenders
- Attracted to Beer

Moth Effect & Impact Characteristics

Out of Season – Moths invested their primary development time underground and in darkness. Why? What happened that motivated the butterfly to the sunlight and plants, while the moth slipped into the dirt? Let's suppose the pressure of life got in the way.

So much time was invested into growing, becoming, wallowing and crawling only to discover the moth was required to shut down again! Perhaps it was exhausted considering another lockdown, isolation, being still held tight, or the patience it takes to become something completely different. I'd imagine that the moth went in the dirt not to be unique but maybe it intended to give up.

But, because God the Divine is the author and designer of all creation, despite the frustration of the moth, nature had another plan. It would not become it's intended plan of a beloved butterfly, but a moth. However, this change of plan redirected the moth's divine appointment with nature, sunlight and the nutrition necessary for the journey. The time in darkness caused a deficiency. Just like Janet Jackson told us, "like a moth to a flame burned by the fire". The moth missed its season of early nutrition with light. Now the moth is drawn with thirst in addition to the wrong light at the wrong time all the time.

Do not miss your appointed seasons. Some opportunities do not offer make up exams. A moth is usually unseen during the day. At night it is drawn to flames and hot bright lights. The moth is constantly running the risk of getting burned or the loss of life. The early decision to run from what was necessary can have lasting negative effects and impact.

Understanding the starting life of a moth is key and critical as you review the next key characteristics of a moth. In the meantime, do not miss your appointed and divine seasons, even if the tasks or calling seems utterly painful, ridiculous or unnecessary. It is all in divine order.

Unattractive – Moths usually appear unattractive. When discovered, most home owners or campers work to exterminate them because they look intimidating like a pest, not admirable like a butterfly. Whether we like it or not, appearance matters. How you appear to others may be instrumental to your success. Let's set aside viral sensations and a certain author. On average, people are attracted to good looking people. A local radio podcast asked for feedback on an opinion poll. "Do attractive people get a pass?"

PAUSE, attractive is simply a description for what best fits you. Do not over extend yourself with unhealthy ambition of over weight loss, wasteful cosmetic surgery and comparing your beauty or looks to others. Just show up at your total best as often as possible when possible, period. On the other hand, attractive isn't just a representation of your physical appearance.

Are you the odd person at the event or in the culture that causes other's uneasiness? Is your personality or behaviors disruptive or intrusive? Is your attempt to be different or stand out turn you into an eyesore rather than art? Sometimes people won't be bothered because you present yourself in an unattractive uneasy manner. Stop blaming others. Everyone is not a hater. Perhaps you or the person you know who fits this description is actually self-sabotaging their brand, name, reputation and ability to engage others. Unattractive behaviors are just as detrimental as an un-kept appearance.

Slippery – Moths tentacles are slippery. They are difficult to hold or touch. When you attempt to put your hands on a moth they tend to slip away easily. When seemingly you cannot make a connection with someone you work with, their actions and behavior may feel slippery. You find yourself feeling ungrounded or insecure. This character may be a sign of someone not to trust.

Excellent Night Vision – Moths have the keen ability to see in deep darkness. They typically eat easy prey, i.e. your valuables such as cotton and silk clothing. As you become an influencer and your profile becomes more popular, someone is watching you and you cannot see them. They can clearly see your movement and the deliciousness of your resources. Sometimes they eat away at your items while you are distracted. I say this not to frighten you, but to make sure you understand that you must have a routine to be on guard. Check your inventory, review your resources, hire help, or utilize tools to help you see what you cannot see on your own.

Blend in the Background – Moths typically have dull flat camouflage colors. This can serve as a disguise. The war by a moth on your merchandise is usually in plain sight. They blend into the interior of your place, things or the nature around you. Their ability to be still, watch while feasting on your inventory is a core characteristic of their behavior. You must be observant of who's around you and on your team.

Great Pretenders – Moths are skilled in mimicking other animals and insects. Sometimes they inflate their wings to appear large like a bird. Other times they cuddle their size to appear small like a worm. As you grow, be sensitive to people that give false appearances. People often present themselves larger than their truth simply to gain access to you and your resources. Some say these people are liars.

Attracted to Beer – Moths like the smell of beer. Sometimes when connecting to certain cultures, tribes or organizations, they have social habits you have to navigate. Alcohol, drugs or other stimulants may be how they do deals, mingle and bond. Don't force your behaviors on others, and be sensitive about being critical of others. You have to decide if the tribe's requirement for drinking, drugging or other intoxication is a fit for your destiny.

As you build relationships with tribe partners, networks, groups, businesses, clubs, peers, co-workers, and other distinguished organizations, your ability to accurately assess others for the benefit of doing good work is essential. The tips of Fraud Influencers and Moth Characteristics are not provided for you to make snap judgements. As you grow and build within your purpose, the journey is a destiny. People-relationships are necessary and not extinct. Despite the fact that automation is rising, and artificial intelligence is the new normal, people are still a key to unlock your potential. Be careful not to surround yourself with those that have the ability to cause severe or irreversible harm to your life. I once heard a quote, "people who have nothing to lose will cause you to lose everything." Understanding tribe culture, norms, isms, expectations, and entry points for acceptance are critical. Stories of scandal in the entertainment industry are rampant. Victims tell horrifying recounts of devastating required sex acts, drug use, and violence. On the other hand, there is still a world of positive people that God has set aside for your good.

When I opened my company, I did not have any immediate family support. I'd burned them out through a prior business. I was on my own. After finalizing my legal structure and launching the first website, that was it. I had a $300 loan from mom, big dreams, and zero clients & prospects. I wish I could tell you that it was all good. Honestly, there were too many days I was in crisis and poverty. Every year, God allowed me to attract people with new resources, ideas, and passion for my work. Some were enemies in disguise, and others were what felt like angels.

Let's talk about my first full-time staff. I'll call him Mr. Cokane. This guy had me hypnotized. He dangled creative solutions. I'm not sure how I didn't spot his incredible ability to lie and steal. Perhaps I was blinded by the white powder in his nose or him sneaking in my office stealing my deodorant, and my clients behind my back. Affiliation with him has lasting scars. Nevertheless, despite unexpected difficulties, God's love story is still being written. Not everyone is your enemy and everything we go through can help us grow (flowers and plants need dirt).

Notes and Reflections

BONUS CHAPTER

GWS
GROW WITH SNOW

How Women Advance at Work

This BONUS chapter shares what women must know about career advancement. These career topics also serve those mentoring women for career advancement at work and the office.

It's true, I worked in corporate industries my entire career before launching the Michelle Snow brand. As a young teenager I applied for the cool jobs at the supermarket, sneaker stores, and fast-food chains, I was denied repeatedly. I really thought something was wrong with me. Why wasn't I good enough for Roy Rogers??? Instead, I was picked for insurance agencies, major banks and pharmaceutical. I thought that was utterly boring.

Eventually, I accepted my path. After graduating high school, I started work at the Pep Boys Corporate Office. From there I had the advantage of working at headquarter offices in major industries. I had a front row seat to the beauty of Corporate America and its secrets.

This chapter is an unreleased question and answer interview with a national media site for executives. In the first question the interviewer asked me to give their readers tips for women on how to advance your career fast in the workplace. I flipped the conversation. I took a wild risk by sharing a raw authentic perspective about the truth about women at work. Buckle up, let's ride while I give you the Best Advice No One Gave Me ©

What are FAST Career Stages at Work and the Office?

F.A.S.T. Results – Forced Alignment to Sink Your Talent! Fast absolutely feels awesome when you arrive at the drive-thru, get in line at the mall, or when the work day seems to move quickly. Ahhh, yes! The sweet sensation of fast is excellent. On the other hand, let's consider the statistics of fast results for major life-changing circumstances. For example, lottery winners are more likely to declare bankruptcy within three-to-five years than the average American (CFPBS).

As a professional, thought-leader and or influencer at work, fast results within your career typically evolves through conquering of many several key stages. These stages are not often taught or mentored to others with transparency. Past generations were forced to learn and apply the follow stages through hardship, missed opportunities and lost careers.

What are Career Stages for Success?

1. **Information** – awareness, knowledge and passion
2. **Application** – skill-building, adaptation, ability to be led
3. **Implementation** – execution and nurturing of relationships
4. **Performance** – credibility, measuring results and outcomes
5. **Decision** – you intentionally or unintentionally…

   - Become content – stop growing, master your role, no desire to advance or accelerate
   - Dream and imagine bigger! However you vacillate in pain, fear and victimization (plateau by choice).
   - Celebrate and appreciate past achievements, actively pursue your desired success goal(s) and reach for success

6. **Grow** – storm, norm, failure, self-reflection, and evaluation

7. **Peak** – performance, credibility, burn your ships of the past, sustain your tribal community, high performance, skills-master, lateral success (ability to pivot), and tribal community reciprocity (significant measurable benefactor of your social investments)
8. **Outcome** – ultimate outcome revealed... fast career advancement

For Women, are there Specific Things to Keep in Mind in Terms of Fast Professional Advancement? Are Things Slightly Different for Women, and if so, Why?

Fast professional advancement is subjective. Women will often experience an expedited journey as career professionals when she learns to appreciate and use her assets that are best for her. She has internal, external, soft and hard skills and capabilities.

Three successful women who often later regret their path:

1. Boys Club Woman

Women have the unique advantage to project themselves as strong, hard, fierce and competitive. Women have at times successfully aligned themselves with men to reduce their presence as a female contender. Women have sacrificed becoming mothers, loving marriages, and the choice to appear emotional or vulnerable. Some may be identified by peers or subordinates as a bully. She may be self-trained in apathy. She leans on apathy simply to survive the brutal culture she's created on her path toward success.

2. Sexy by Nature

There are women that emphatically embrace their natural qualities as a woman by using their sexuality to climb to the peak of success. The woman who rides the back of her sexuality emphasizes and struts her curves, soft touch and pretty appearance. This woman is known to swap sexual favors as a bargaining tool for her distinct vision of success. She's daring, takes risks and perhaps has found a path to manipulate ethics, rules and some may say morality. She knows the boss is married yet she feeds his (or her) ego with the gravitas of lust fulfilled. As an excellent actress, she may appear helpful, supportive and engaged. On the other hand she may be confident that a quality business performance is unnecessary because her sexual bargaining has purchased her success.

3. Girl Friday

She's known to everyone as the one who'll finish and clean up our mess. This woman has slipped into the trap of becoming the mom of the office. Some identify her as a people pleaser. She may feel like the doormat of the team. She's constantly making the effort to keep everyone successful, pleased and happy except for herself. She often says yes to work, projects and responsibilities even while silently at the tipping point of total self-destruction.

The yes girl has convinced herself that through her track record of consistency, excellent outcomes and stellar performances, she's the only one to get the job done. She may unconsciously sabotage her peace with performance workaholism. She redefines this behavior as reliability or passion. Unfortunately this woman may be a closet addict of obsessive compulsive behaviors like drugs or alcohol. If she's able to avoid substance abuse, she may be overly zealous within her religious affairs or meddling in the affairs of those around her.

Many career women find true success when they accept that being a woman at work is both her weapon and her super power. She's born with an innate ability to multi-serve, code switch, demonstrate emotion, be sweet, soft, feminine, and courageous all while being brilliant. When she matures she accepts, in the words of Chaka Khan and Whitney Houston, that she is "every woman." However, she would be foolish to pretend to be every woman all the time and in every circumstance. It is critical to choose what woman she is and when. For best results and the most successful outcomes, she decides daily what woman is necessary for that day, task, and in her life.

Five Secrets of a Successful Career Woman (On a Faster than Average Path)

Women who tend to advance swiftly in their careers typically appreciate the necessity of seedtime, harvest, and are laser focused on the ultimate expected outcome. She has embraced her vision as reality and is keenly aware that every decision may impede or impact her ultimate goal(s). She aligns her personal and daily habits to carry her vision like cargo. In addition, she masters her skill-capabilities, and takes responsibility for her failures and successes. Her words are guarded. This career woman does not become bitter, gossip or despair. Her experience has taught her that failure is a lesson in action.

Failure is not permission to quit. In the words of Donavan West, "She listens to lead." Her greatest competitor lives within her mind, not the office next door. She traded competition for industry and workplace peers. She sets ambitious vision success dates. She's inspired, not absurd. Career women advancing swiftly understand that time is relative to her abilities and beliefs. She's her own woman, but is courageous enough to genuinely celebrate the success of those around her.

Summary Secrets

1. She is unapologetic about her spirituality, faith and the energy she attracts into her life.
2. At times she will painfully compromise today's wins for the benefit of tomorrow's legacy.
3. She is NOT a right-fighter. She is confident enough to not try to prove she is right in every circumstance. Often her work will speak louder than her voice.
4. She creates and maintains strong respectful relationships of reciprocity within her peer group and her leaders.
5. She has learned that as much as she wants what is in front of her, she may also have to leave it behind her.

Notes and Reflections

Notes and Reflections

Notes and Reflections

Bibliography

Chan, G. (2019). *Eight Colors That Will Brightly Grow Your Personal Brand.* https://www.forbes.com/sites/goldiechan /2019/09/17/ eight-colors-that-will-brightly-grow-your-personal-brand/?sh=8f-f5ec8255ac

Sauter, M., Comen, M., Frohlich, T., and Stebbins, S. (2018). *When Product Launches Go Awry: 50 Worst Product Flops of All Time.* https://www.usatoday.com/story/money/2018/07/11/50-worst-product-flops-of-all-time/36734837/

Nearly one-third of lottery winners eventually declare bankruptcy (CFPBS). *ryanhart.org December 3, 2018*

ACKNOWLEDGEMENTS

GWS

GROW WITH SNOW

I am grateful to everyone that participated on this journey. Counting names will never fit into one book, and certainly not one page. My core original team of coaches Jakki Grant who first said, "You are a motivational speaker". I said, what is that? Richard Washington, and Donavan West taught me the art of serving people. Thank you, Jeneen Barlow, who taught me that I was different. You escorted me into my ability to recognize and accept my purpose in marketplace services.

My alumni, Peirce College and my high school, Samuel S. Fels. You helped me learn how to make character an action word. Your actions yesterday inspire me towards excellence today.

Thank you to the many churches and denominations that helped me develop transferrable skills. Reading church announcements, coordinating services, teaching classes, singing on teams, coaching committees and working in the kitchen were all instrumental in my ability to develop both people and leadership skills. The cornerstone of my success is owed to the Church of God in Christ (COGIC), and the Baptist Church. Also, Bishop Derrick Hanna was critical in my ability to heal from personal, spiritual, social, emotional, and spiritual pain. He was instrumental in being the rock that taught me how to deliver coach-consulting services. His church was my first business audience for the Michelle Snow brand.

Thank you to my team! Although I missed all your deadlines, you stayed committed.

Ultimately, thank you to Michelle Snow Network and the Grow With Snow VIP Community. You are legion; I cannot name you personally. But you must know that I AM BECAUSE YOU ARE!

GWS
GROW WITH SNOW